Pondering Nativity

Jean Andrianoff

ISBN: 9798376730355

DEDICATION

To my husband, David Andrianoff, who over the past 50 plus years has expanded my horizons, motivating and encouraging me as we explored the world together.

CONTENTS

ACKNOWLEDGMENTS

In creating man in His image, God offered mankind the joy of creating. The nativity sets pictured here reflect that creativity expressed through various media by craftsmen and women throughout the world. I am grateful to each one whose hands fashioned these sets.

Thanks to my husband, David Andrianoff, who encouraged the creation of our nativity set collection, purchasing sets as he travelled, whether I was with him or not. He also consistently encourages me in my writing and publishing efforts, patiently editing countless editions of my manuscripts.

Thank you to Word Ways, my sisters in faith and writing, who uphold, encourage, and sustain me with their prayers and love.

Chapter 13, "Chosen Ones," was originally published in the blog *Godspace* on December 16, 2014. The blog, founded and facilitated by Christine Sine, may be accessed at godspacelight.com.

Above all, praise and glory to the triune God Who took on human flesh, entering the world as Immanuel, God with us.

Introduction

In these devotionals, I have paired passages in Matthew, Luke, and John that relate the birth and origins of Jesus with illustrations from our collection of nativity sets from around the world.

We did not consciously decide to collect nativity sets, but as they began to accumulate, we sought them more intentionally. We searched for nativity sets in the different countries we visited; if we found none, we put together a family unit of local figurines. In Central Asia, figures of camels and sages in traditional dress became sets of wise men.

We do not see our sets as objects of worship and most are not biblically accurate, generally including shepherds and wise men gathered at the same point in time. The physical characteristics and dress of the figures reflect the country and culture of their origin.

In spite of these limitations, I found new insights into the story of Jesus' birth and its application to my life as I reflected on the biblical birth narratives alongside the various nativity sets in our collection. Pondering the incarnation this way has given me a fuller appreciation of this reality:

> *Christ Jesus, who, though he was in the form of God, did not count equality with God a thing to be grasped, but emptied himself, by taking the form of a servant, being born in the likeness of men.*
> Philippians 2: 5-7

The series begins on December 1 and continues through Epiphany, January 6. Though the number of days in Advent in the liturgical calendar varies, I have chosen to follow the often-used convention of offering 25 Advent devotionals, one for each day of December up to Christmas.

I pray that these meditations will help direct your focus on Jesus during Advent and Christmas.

December 1 - **Interruptions**

In the sixth month the angel Gabriel was sent from God to a city of Galilee named Nazareth, to a virgin betrothed to a man whose name was Joseph, of the house of David. And the virgin's name was Mary. Luke 1:26, 27

One of my favorite nativity sets is the matryoshka set we bought in Tashkent, Uzbekistan. Its character reflects the Russian influence during the Soviet era on this predominately Muslim country.

The outermost shell depicts the angel's appearance to Mary. Sometimes we leave the set encased for a while to focus on the beginning of the narrative, though of course the story actually began much earlier, long before Mary's birth or even before the creation of the earth, a plan God ordained from eternity.

Luke introduces us very simply to the young woman who will play a significant role not only in the Christmas story, but in the history of mankind as well—a Nazarene maiden named Mary. All he tells us about her is that she is the fiancée of a man named Joseph, a descendant of King David.

Imagine Mary's amazement as an angel greets her—an occurrence no more common in Mary's day than in our own. God had been silent for several hundred years. People still believed in a coming Messiah, but with the similar belief we hold in relation to Jesus' return. Yes, we believe, and yes, we affirm that it could be today; but we go about our daily tasks and plan for the future, not really expecting to be interrupted by ruptured clouds. Mary, however, was ready. In spite of her surprise, she had the faith to believe that God would keep His promises and that process might involve His breaking into her own life.

May we live this Advent season in a sense of expectation, ready for anything from the dramatic return of Christ in glory to the more mundane interruptions of our daily routine as Jesus appears in the guise of a needy neighbor.

December 2 – **Favored of God**

And he came to her and said, "Greetings, O favored one, the Lord is with you!" But she was greatly troubled at the saying, and tried to discern what sort of greeting this might be. Luke 1:28-29

When we think of Christmas angels, we often visualize a cherubic toddler, blond curls encircled in a tinsel halo. Surely this is far from the vision Mary saw as she gazed fearfully at the angel Gabriel. This Kenyan nativity set, with its bearded angel, may more accurately depict the being Mary faced in her Nazarene courtyard. Others who had seen Gabriel felt a great sense of fear and awe. Daniel fell on his face in terror when Gabriel first appeared to him. Zechariah was left speechless after Gabriel identified himself as one who stands "in the presence of God." Gabriel, special herald of God, appeared only when God had a supremely important message to convey. And here he stood, greeting a simple Nazarene maiden as "O favored one!" Who wouldn't be "greatly troubled at the saying?"

In our materialistic society, we think of God's favor as bestowing good things, such as health and wealth. Or we may move beyond that to perceiving His favor as spiritual blessing. But we rarely consider God's favor an opportunity to share in hardship and suffering. Yes, God blessed Mary with the honor of becoming the mother of God incarnate, but it involved much pain, both in the immediate disgrace of an out-of-wedlock pregnancy and in the ultimate horror of watching her firstborn son die a painful and humiliating death. But favored she was, significant enough that God sent Gabriel from His presence to communicate her special status.

May we accept the privileges and responsibilities of the favor God has shown us with the grace and humility shown by Mary.

December 3 – **Do Not Fear**

And the angel said to her, "Do not be afraid, Mary, for you have found favor with God. And behold, you will conceive in your womb and bear a son, and you shall call his name Jesus. He will be great and will be called the Son of the Most High. And the Lord God will give to him the throne of his father David, and he will reign over the house of Jacob forever, and of his kingdom there will be no end." Luke 1:30-33

When God sends an angelic messenger, the message often begins with, "Do not fear." The instinctive human reaction to something so out of the ordinary is terror. Mary reacted to Gabriel's greeting with apprehension, and Gabriel hastened to assure her that he brought good news. He began with a personal reassurance to Mary that she had found favor with God. This was not a visit of judgment, but of commendation.

Gabriel continued with practical instructions—the name for the baby. More than a simple appellation, the name held prophetic meaning, describing the baby's very identity.

As the angel went on, Mary might have needed a few more "Do not fear's." He told this simple village maiden that her child would be called God's Son and that He would rule on David's throne in a never-ending kingdom. I think I would feel increasing apprehension rather than comfort! What an enormous sense of responsibility Mary must have felt about her task.

But Gabriel didn't tell Mary, "If you do everything right and are a perfect mother, this child will fulfill all these promises." His initial "Do not fear" carried the implication that God would take care of keeping the promises. God would see that the child fulfilled all He foretold.

We have a lovely Vietnamese nativity set carved of stone—a lasting medium, a good symbol of a "kingdom with no end." The figure of the baby with its arms stretched out perpendicular to the body seems also prophetic of what this child would ultimately endure on His way to providing the salvation His name implied and to attaining the everlasting kingdom promised by Gabriel. At this point Mary did not know all that the promise would entail, but the angel's words were adequate for her and for us: "Do not fear."

December 4 – **God of the Impossible**

And Mary said to the angel, "How will this be, since I am a virgin?"

And the angel answered her, "the Holy Spirit will come upon you, and the power of the Most High will overshadow you; therefore the child to be born will be called holy—the Son of God. And behold, your relative Elizabeth in her old age has also conceived a son, and this is the sixth month with her who was called barren. For nothing will be impossible with God." Luke 1:34-37

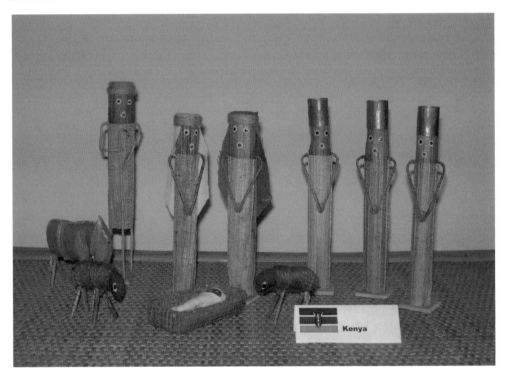

We have two nativity sets from Kenya: one beautifully carved from smooth wood; the other crafted from tubes of banana fiber. This rather roughly crafted set delights me because of the expressions on the faces of each figure. The mouths are red dots outlined in white—perfect round "O's"—giving the characters a look of perpetual surprise. The eyes—black dots outlined in white—reinforce the astonished look. No more skillful carving or painting could so perfectly express the wonder we should feel at what took place in the nativity. What? A virgin is having a baby? And He is the Son of God? Is this not cause for amazement?

Isaiah had prophesied that a virgin would bear a child, but we can certainly forgive Mary for not relating this to the angel's strange announcement that she was going to have a baby. Mary knew that virgins do not bear children. It had never happened and was beyond the range of human possibility. Mary felt startled and perplexed.

The angel gave Mary the basic information she needed to accept this child by faith—she would conceive the child through the power of God Most High. And the child would be the very Son of God. For a bit of concrete evidence of God's power the angel added the news that barren Elizabeth had also conceived a child in her old age and added the explanation, "For nothing will be impossible with God."

We so often hear this part of the story that we either take it for granted or dismiss it as fable. But shouldn't we respond with the wonder expressed on the faces of the Kenyan figures—with absolute, stunned awe? God is the God of the impossible—He gives a son to a virgin, He offers forgiveness to the guilty, and He raises the dead to life. What a comfort to know that no matter how difficult the circumstances we face, we serve the God of the impossible! A God with the power to give a virgin a child can meet any need. No matter how orthodox our beliefs, how great our faith, or how high our expectation of God, an exclamation of "Wow!" is still an appropriate response to God's miraculous work in Mary's life or in ours.

December 5 - **Obedience**

And Mary said, "Behold I am the servant of the Lord; let it be to me according to your word." And the angel departed from her. Luke 1:38

We often claim that if we only knew the will of God for our lives or for a particular decision we face, we would happily obey. We want to do God's will and would if we only knew what He wanted. Yet would it really be that simple?

The men and women in the Bible chosen by God for a particular task had varied responses to God's direction. Abraham's response was to go "as the Lord had told him." Moses, on the other hand, negotiated with God, worrying about his imperfect communication skills and whether people would believe him. Gideon struggled to believe that God would really use him. A clear and direct heavenly communication does not necessarily signify a willing and obedient response.

Mary's reply to her angelic visitor provides one of the clearest and most immediate positive responses to a divine mandate. She perceived her relationship to God as one of service and obedience. She believed the angel's words, expressing a willingness to assume the role that God asked her to play—no negotiating or questioning.

Our nativity set from Mongolia is carved from wood—a rare commodity in a land covered with miles of treeless steppes. The figure of Mary in this set conveys a posture of willing obedience. Just as the wood submitted itself to the hand of the carver, so Mary submitted to God's plan for her, a plan that would impact not just her own life, but all human history. I need reminding of Mary's ready obedience to allow it "to be to me according to your word."

December 6 - **Connections**

In those days Mary arose and went with haste into the hill country, to a town in Judah, and she entered the house of Zechariah and greeted Elizabeth. And when Elizabeth heard the greeting of Mary, the baby leaped in her womb. And Elizabeth was filled with the Holy Spirit, and she exclaimed with a loud cry, "Blessed are you among women, and blessed is the fruit of your womb! And why is this granted to me that the mother of my Lord should come to me? For behold, when the sound of your greeting came to my ears, the baby in my womb leaped for joy. And blessed is she who believed that there would be a fulfillment of what was spoken to her from the Lord." Luke 1:39-45

Cyprus

For years, I dreamed of visiting Cyprus with my brothers to see the place of their birth, the land where my father ministered for over a decade. When my oldest brother told me that he planned to visit Cyprus with a group organized by our mutual alma mater, I signed on. Visiting places where my family had lived and worked gave me a sense of connection to a part of family history that had previously been only an abstraction In my mind. Seeing, hearing, smelling, touching and tasting Cyprus deepened my link with my family's experiences.

While we purchased both the nativity triptych and the little donkey in Cyprus, probably only the donkey was locally made. Donkeys have played a vital role in the agricultural economy of the Island for thousands of years. And though the Bible doesn't give us this information, we often assume that Mary traveled to Bethlehem on a donkey. Our little fabric donkey holds a connection for us to both the nativity story and the Island of Cyprus.

We often downplay the physical, material world, feeling that the need for these connections is somehow not very spiritual. Yet God provided such links for Mary at the time when she may have needed something tangible to reassure her of the reality of her angelic experience. The angel told Mary the news of Elizabeth's pregnancy. Mary responded by traveling "with haste" to visit Elizabeth. The actuality of Elizabeth's pregnancy and the Spirit-filled words of Elizabeth confirmed to Mary the truth of the angel's words. Elizabeth and Mary, though years apart in age, found their experiences of miraculous pregnancies and the anticipation of raising unique sons connected them. The three months they spent together must have created a very strong bond.

God rarely asks us to deal with life's challenges without human support. He often gives us connections to affirm and strengthen us. During this Advent season, let's remember to thank Him for such connections in our own lives and to ask for a willingness to serve others in need of human support.

December 7 – O**f Humble Estate**

And Mary said,

"My soul magnifies the Lord,
  and my spirit rejoices in God my Savior,
for he has looked on the humble estate of his servant.
  For behold, from now on all generations will call me blessed;
for he who is mighty has done great things for me,
  and holy is his name.
And his mercy is for those who fear him
  from generation to generation.
He has shown strength with his arm;
  he has scattered the proud in the thoughts of their hearts;
he has brought down the mighty from their thrones
  and exalted those of humble estate;
he has filled the hungry with good things,
  and the rich he has sent away empty.
He has helped his servant Israel,
  in remembrance of his mercy,
as he spoke to our fathers,
  to Abraham and to his offspring forever."

And Mary remained with her about three months and returned to her home.

Luke 1:46-56

The words that Mary spoke to Elizabeth describe both her own sense of humility and a sense of praise for God's greatness. She does not boast that "all generations will call me blessed" because of what she has done, but because of what God has done for her. Much of Mary's song, generally known as the Magnificat, is quoted from the Old Testament, words that Mary must have heard as part of her cultural heritage. Yet the emphasis is revolutionary—the favor God bestows on the poor and disadvantaged, with the example of Mary's own elevation from her lowly status to the mother of the King of Kings. Her theme permeates the ministry of her son: God cares about the poor.

The Vietnamese nativity figures carved from tree roots illustrate this passage of Scripture well. What lowlier medium exists for sculpting figures? Yet from the humble roots emerge lovely human forms, objects to help us reflect on the man and woman God chose to parent His Son. The sculptor has taken an ordinary tree root and carved out likenesses of humans, the crowning glory of creation.

The use of the root has significance for other reasons: Jesus is prophesied as "the root of Jesse." From the family tree of Jesse and David, through a poor servant girl, God sends blessing and redemption to mankind. The root reminds us not only of Jesus' royal family tree, but also of His lowly beginnings. Through the poor, the world is blessed. If God cares this much for the poor, can we do any less? In what ways can we faithfully serve God by serving the disadvantaged among us during this Christmas season?

December 8 – **Finding Your Voice**

And his father Zechariah was filled with the Holy Spirit and prophesied, saying,

> *"Blessed be the Lord God of Israel,*
> *for he has visited and redeemed his people*
> *and has raised up a horn of salvation for us*
> *in the house of his servant David,*
> *as he spoke by the mouth of his holy prophets from of old,*
> *that we should be saved from our enemies*
> *and from the hand of all who hate us;*
> *to show the mercy promised to our fathers*
> *and to remember his holy covenant,*
> *the oath that he swore to our father Abraham, to grant us*
> *that we, being delivered from the hand of our enemies,*
> *might serve him without fear,*
> *in holiness and righteousness before him all our days.*

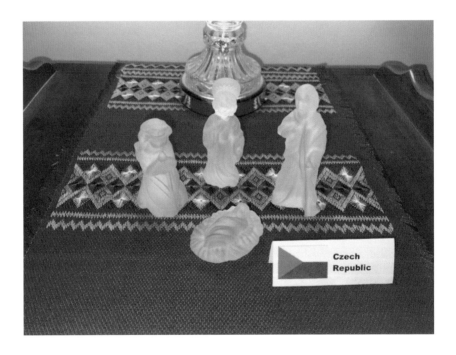

And you, child, will be called the prophet of the Most High;
 for you will go before the Lord to prepare his ways,
to give knowledge of salvation to his people
 in the forgiveness of their sins,
because of the tender mercy of our God,
 whereby the sunrise shall visit us from on high
to give light to those who sit in darkness and in the shadow of death,
 to guide our feet into the way of peace." Luke 1:67-79

When Mary visited Elizabeth after learning of her pregnancy, both women poured out words of prophecy and praise. No doubt Mary's three-month visit also included girl talk of pregnancy symptoms and plans for the expected babies. Throughout this time, Elizabeth's husband, old Zechariah, struck dumb when he doubted the angel's announcement that he was about to become a father, remained silent. After Mary left, Elizabeth's house must have felt eerily quiet until at last, the promised child arrived. Apparently, Zechariah and Elizabeth had managed to communicate in some way, because Elizabeth knew to give the baby the name John. When the family would not take her word for it, Zechariah motioned for a writing tablet and wrote, "His name is John." This act of faith released Zechariah's long-silent tongue and he erupted with a flow of words—words given him by the Holy Spirit.

Not only did Zechariah prophesy about the role of his son, but he also spoke of the soon-to-be-born cousin whose path John would prepare. His words tell of deliverance and salvation, forgiveness and peace, and of the light this child would bring into the world.

Our Bohemian glass figurines from the Czech Republic seem illuminated by nearby light. Light transforms their translucence. Without a source of light, their surface simply looks a bit frosty. Illuminated, they glow. Similarly, the world without Jesus remained dark, but with the visit of the "sunrise from on high," our darkness turned to light.

We seldom include Zechariah's words in our telling of the Christmas story, yet they build expectation of the significance of the child who will soon be born. God used an angel as well as the prophetic voices of women and men to prepare the world for the coming advent. Zechariah found his voice to proclaim God's salvation. Have you found yours?

December 9 – **A Just Man**

Now the birth of Jesus Christ took place in this way. When his mother Mary had been betrothed to Joseph, before they came together she was found to be with child from the Holy Spirit. And her husband Joseph, being a just man and unwilling to put her to shame, resolved to divorce her quietly. But as he considered these things, behold, an angel of the Lord appeared to him in a dream, saying, "Joseph, son of David, do not fear to take Mary as your wife, for that which is conceived in her is from the Holy Spirit. She will bear a son, and you shall call his name Jesus, for he will save his people from their sins. Matthew 1:18-21

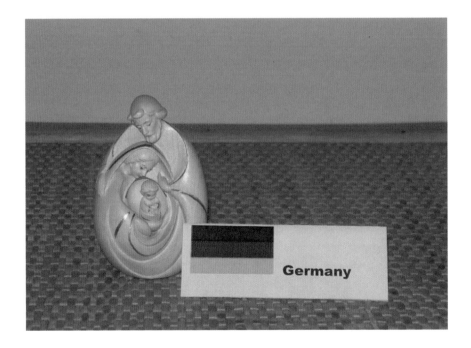

How disturbed Joseph must have felt when he learned that Mary was pregnant! He must have felt confused, betrayed, disappointed, and hurt. He knew that he was not the father of her child, and no doubt questioned Mary's explanation of angels and miraculous conception—how better for a young woman to justify a pregnancy to her fiancé? His skepticism extended to his decision to divorce Mary—to release her from their marriage contract. He had every right to accuse Mary publicly and even to have her stoned, but Matthew tells us Joseph was "a just man." This provides our first indication of the character of the man who would act as Jesus' earthly father, a man of mercy more interested in showing kindness than vengeance. Rather than acting in haste, he "considered these things."

As Joseph pondered what he should do, God intervened, giving Joseph his own angelic visitation through a dream. The angel confirmed the truth of Mary's claims about the miraculous nature of her pregnancy and of God's special purpose for this child. Joseph's reaction to the dream underscores his strength of character. He believed the angel and put aside his doubts and fears to make Mary his wife.

The exquisitely carved figure a friend brought us from Germany portrays the role that Joseph assumed in making Mary his wife, that of loving provider and protector of this young woman and her child. God's choice of Joseph was as critical as His choice of Mary in supplying parents for His Son's earthly home. We see God's own attributes of mercy and faithfulness reflected in the character of this "just man."

December 10 – **God with Us**

All this took place to fulfill what the Lord had spoken by the prophet:

"Behold, the virgin shall conceive and bear a son,
and they shall call his name Immanuel!"

(which means, God with us). When Joseph woke from sleep, he did as the
angel of the Lord commanded him: he took his wife, but knew her not until
she had given birth to a son. And he called his name Jesus.

Matthew 1:22-25

Throughout his gospel, Matthew sought to make the connections for his Jewish readers between prophecy and its fulfillment in the life of Jesus. Matthew tied the words of Isaiah's prophecy regarding the long-awaited Messiah to the angel's message. Perhaps Joseph, too, remembered these familiar words, giving him a deeper understanding of Mary's claims to a supernatural pregnancy. No longer did he debate about whether to make her his wife. He believed the words of the angel and acted in obedience to the angel's command.

Not only did the angel's words assure Joseph of the reason for Mary's pregnancy, they also helped him to understand something of the nature of the child she would bear. This child would be Immanuel—God with us. We use the theological term "incarnation" to describe God's taking on human flesh in order to live among us. As Joseph pondered the meaning of Mary's pregnancy, in her womb God was developing muscles and bones, just like any other infant.

Our nativity set from Hungary contains only Jesus's nuclear family—just Mary and Joseph and the baby—before the arrival of shepherds and angels and Magi. This family began as Joseph obeyed the angel's command to take Mary as his wife, as God Himself took on flesh and blood and bones to come and live among us. Immanuel!

December 11 – **Of the House of David**

In those days a decree went out from Caesar Augustus that all the world should be registered. This was the first registration when Quirinius was governor of Syria. And all went to be registered, each to his own town. And Joseph also went up from Galilee, from the town of Nazareth, to Judea, to the city of David, which is called Bethlehem, because he was of the house and lineage of David, to be registered with Mary, his betrothed, who was with child. Luke 2:1-5

Pewter is probably the costliest material used to create any of the nativity sets in our collection. Royal Selangor Pewter, a name derived through an endorsement from His Royal Highness the Sultan of Selangor, Malaysia, created this set.

Mary and Joseph's descent from the royal house of David compelled them to undertake their journey to Bethlehem, the royal city of David. Their royal roots must have seemed to Mary and Joseph more of a burden than an asset at this time. They must have wondered why God allowed this situation to arise at such a critical time. Shouldn't God have smoothed the way for an easy birth for this special child? Shouldn't He have rewarded their willing obedience with a measure of ease?

Sometimes we wonder about difficulties in our own lives. As royalty—children of the King—shouldn't we expect certain privileges? In our minds, that translates to problems easily overcome, if they arise at all. Yet God, who rules over the nations, permitted an arduous journey for the parents of this royal child.

Ironically, the Roman emperor who saw himself as holding supreme authority over the lives of others, served the plan God had designed from eternity, placing Mary and Joseph in Bethlehem for the birth of His Son. The emperor was aware neither of the sovereignty of God that granted him the authority he enjoyed, nor of the royal birth taking place in a far province of his empire. There the prophecy of Isaiah would be fulfilled regarding the king who would occupy David's throne forever:

> *For to us a child is born, to us a son is given; and the government shall be upon his shoulder . . . of the increase of his government and of peace there will be no end, on the throne of David and over his kingdom, to establish it and to uphold it with justice and with righteousness from this time forth and forevermore.* Isaiah 9:6-7

December 12 – **The Fullness of Time**

And while they were there, the time came for her to give birth. And she gave birth to her firstborn son and wrapped him in swaddling cloths and laid him in a manger, because there was no place for them in the inn. Luke 2:6-7

My favorite part of our Lao nativity set is the house, a miniature version of a Lao village home of bamboo and thatch. Millions of Lao babies have been born in similar homes, a setting far more similar to the place of Jesus' birth than our sterile, modern hospitals or birthing centers. In the still moments after the birth, Mary may have listened to the soft crunching of the livestock munching hay and the quiet rustling of their movements. The sweet scent of fresh hay no doubt mingled with the pungent odor of animal dung as the crisp night air drifted into the stable. Only starlight or possibly a dim lantern penetrated the night's blackness. All these sensations would be familiar to a Lao mother in her home above the family's livestock.

Many women around the world continue to give birth in similarly humble settings. God could have selected more privileged circumstances for the birth of His Son, but instead chose to identify with the poor. Even if Mary had been permitted to give birth in her own humble home, her situation would have been easier. Yet God chose this particular time and place.

The Fullness of Time

Over the roads dusty and brown
They made their way to Bethlehem town.
The journey was hard, and the road was long,
And I wonder if Mary felt something was wrong.
Surely not this hour; surely not this place
For your Son to enter time and space.

O, Lord, not this time; oh, Lord, not today.
Can't we first find a better place to stay?
Oh, Lord, not this place, in a pile of hay
With family and friends so far away.

But **when the time had fully come**,
God sent his Son, born of a woman . . .
That we might receive the full rights of sons.

Lord, help me to see that your timing is best,
And as your child, in your time to rest.

December 13 – **Chosen Ones**

And in the same region there were shepherds out in the field, keeping watch over their flock by night. And an angel of the Lord appeared to them, and the glory of the Lord shone around them, and they were filled with great fear. Luke 2:8-9

Imagine your feelings as a shepherd, mechanically carrying out your night watch—probably a little cold, a little bored, listening to the snuffling and bleating of the sheep, trying to stay alert for any indications of impending danger, but not really expecting so much as a fox to scuttle past the flock. Then suddenly the darkness and stillness of the night is shattered by the glorious appearance of an angel of the Lord—an event no more anticipated in the shepherd's daydreams than in ours. No wonder, as the King James Version puts it, "they were sore afraid."

In most of our nativity sets, the shepherds lean placidly on their staffs gazing serenely at the infant Jesus. I like the posture of the shepherd in this Sri Lankan set, as he doffs his hat (yes, he has a hat!) and kneels in reverence beneath the descending angel. He responds in submission to the sudden glory that has overtaken him and his companions as they carry out their ordinary and lowly tasks.

In our modern world we tend to sanitize and glorify the occupation of a shepherd, picturing a gentle man clothed in pristine white robes, holding an equally immaculate and placid lamb. No dirt and no odor. The lamb does not squirm or struggle. Yet shepherds in first century Palestine were a despised class. They lived outside with the sheep, and most likely did not bother with the niceties of bathing and tooth brushing. And shepherds, in spite of the responsibility their profession required, were often regarded as disreputable and dishonest.

Again, God chose to honor those of low esteem in human terms by entrusting the shepherds with the first announcement of His Son's birth. The angel did not appear to the priests in the temple, but to the shepherds in the fields. God seems blissfully oblivious to our human prejudices and social structures. As Paul says in I Corinthians 1:26-29:

> *For consider your calling, brothers: not many of you were wise according to worldly standards, not many were powerful, not many were of noble birth. But God chose what is foolish in the world to shame the wise; God chose what is weak in the world to shame the strong. God chose what is low and despised in the world . . . so that no human being might boast in the presence of God.*

If God has blessed you with the gift of belief in His Son, count yourself in the company of the shepherds, chosen not because of your status or competence or goodness, but simply gifted with grace.

December 14 – **News of Great Joy**

And the angel said to them, "Fear not, for behold, I bring you good news of great joy that will be for all the people." Luke 2:10

Our nativity readings so far have recounted three angelic visitations, and the first words of these messengers included the admonition: "Fear not." God understands that mere mortals, unaccustomed to heavenly visitors, need immediate reassurance. In this case, shepherds needed the reminder that all was well.

In fact, all was not just "well," but great! The angel had good news that would provide abundant joy for all. The news was not just for the shepherds, but for all people. The shepherds faithfully proclaimed this news so that it eventually spread through the region of Bethlehem, then onward to the whole world.

Perhaps you can guess from the shape of our American-purchased Mary and Joseph that they are actually a pair of bells. Bells have long been seen as a symbol of Christmas, and we think of Christmas bells proclaiming the joy of Christ's birth.

For years, church bells have proclaimed celebration at Christmas and weddings, while also pealing solemnly for funerals and tolling the hours to announce the ordinary passing of time. During the Civil War, the poet Henry Wadsworth Longfellow wrestled with the disparity of joyfully ringing Christmas bells at a time of such national division, writing:

> And in despair I bowed my head;
> "There is no peace on earth," I said;
> "For hate is strong,
> And mocks the song
> Of peace on earth, good-will to men!"
>
> Then pealed the bells more loud and deep:
> "God is not dead, nor doth He sleep;
> The Wrong shall fail,
> The Right prevail,
> With peace on earth, good-will to men."

Christmas, a time of great joy, can also be a time of emotional pain for the lonely, stress for the busy, and disappointment for the disadvantaged. What can I do this Advent/Christmas season to bring the hope and joy of Jesus to those experiencing difficult times?

December 15 – **Links of Grace**

For unto you is born this day in the city of David a Savior, who is Christ the Lord. Luke 2:11

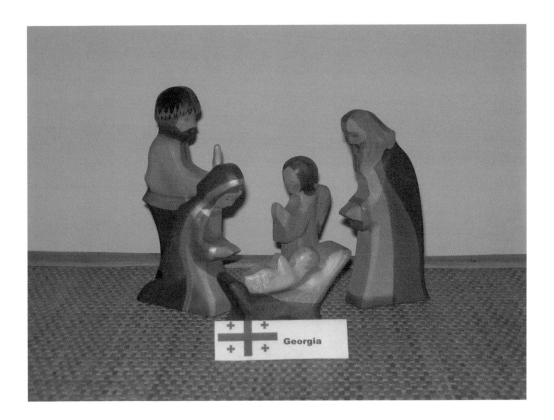

The angel had told the shepherds he brought good news. Now the angel proclaims the specifics of that news: a Savior is born! Shepherds working near David's city, people who shared David's original occupation and humble roots, heard the news first. The shepherds may not have been educated or well versed in the Old Testament, but all in their culture were so infused with the hope of a Savior Messiah that they would have understood the angel's words as a fulfillment of that expectation. At long last God's promise had come true! They no doubt anticipated an end to their own personal suffering. At the very least it surely promised freedom from the tyranny of Rome. Whatever the particulars, the angel brought very good news indeed—news that would extend beyond the shepherds' imagining to offer hope to all mankind.

The shepherd in our nativity set from the Republic of Georgia wears the outfit of a traditional Georgian shepherd. A contemporary Georgian herder of sheep might well wear similar apparel. The salvation brought about by this newborn child stretches back from his ancestor David up through and beyond present-day individuals, whether herding sheep on a Georgian hillside or designing computer software in an elegant office building in Los Angeles. The Savior is for all times and all people.

Links of Grace

In a lonely field
shepherd David plays his harp
and sings of God's grace.

Near David's city
angels proclaim salvation
to startled shepherds.

On Georgian hillsides
shepherds trust the salvation
David's son procured.

December 16 – **A Sign in the Dust**

"And this will be a sign for you: you will find a baby wrapped in swaddling cloths and lying in a manger." Luke 2:12

God, aware of our human tendency to skepticism, often offers signs to confirm His word, even when we haven't asked. He offered Mary the confirmation of Elizabeth's miraculous pregnancy. Isaiah had prophesied the virgin birth itself as a sign from God: "Therefore the Lord himself will give you a sign. Behold, the virgin shall conceive and bear a son, and shall call his name Immanuel" (Isaiah 7:14).

To verify the truth of his announcement to the shepherds, the angel offered a sign consisting of three elements: the baby, the swaddling clothes, and the manger. A newborn baby wrapped in swaddling clothes would not in itself be miraculous—newborns were typically bound in this way. A newborn in a manger, however, would not only be unique, but would also be in stark contrast to the dramatic announcement just made by the angel. The shepherds no doubt expected the long-awaited Messiah to make a spectacular appearance in a noble setting. They would not look for this child among the livestock. But finding a newborn lying in an animal's feeding trough would affirm what the angel had just told them.

Our nativity set from Bangladesh, one of the most densely populated and poorest nations of the world, is sculpted from terra cotta. Terra cotta—literally "baked earth" provides a fitting substance to illustrate the lowly setting of Jesus' birth. Earth—or "dust"—also describes the material from which God created us. Beginning in Genesis the Bible often refers to man as "dust" or "from dust." In Job 10:9, Job asks God, "Remember that you have made me like clay; and will you return me to the dust?" This nativity set is constructed from the very material the Bible identifies with humankind, an apt symbol of Jesus' humanity. Not only is dust described as the material of our origins, but of our ultimate destiny as well, as the Bible speaks of our returning to the dust. Jesus, like all humans, experienced death; yet Jesus became the first one to experience resurrection, releasing mankind from our hopeless dust-bound destiny. Though strips of cloth swaddled him as an infant, the strips that bound him in burial could not contain his resurrected body.

Jesus took on humanity in humble circumstances, an occurrence so humanly unpredictable that it had to be pointed out to the shepherds. Yet, as Paul tells us, He did this for us: "For you know the grace of our Lord Jesus Christ, that though he was rich, yet for your sake he became poor, so that you by his poverty might become rich" (2 Corinthian 8:9). Praise God for His gift of grace clothed in dust!

December 17 – **Glory to God**

And suddenly there was with the angel a multitude of the heavenly host praising God and saying,

> *"Glory to God in the highest, and on earth peace among those with whom he is pleased!"*

Luke 2:13-14

At last, the kind of celestial spectacular we would expect with the arrival of God's Son! The elements of the story so far have been earth-bound and understated—a peasant husband and wife trudging to Bethlehem, a child's birth in a stable, shepherds caring for their sheep. Now heaven can no longer contain itself and erupts with "a multitude of the heavenly host." We can almost imagine the angels begging for release to celebrate this momentous occasion that has received so little proper attention.

Many artists have attempted to portray the awe and joy inspired by the appearance of this heavenly chorus. To me, the abaca fiber angels created by an anonymous Philippine craftsman deserve their place among such works for capturing the sense of jubilation the angels displayed. Even the fragility of the fiber exhibits the ethereal substance of the angelic beings. The curling fibers on the angels' billowing skirts could be part of their clothing or part of the clouds. While the real angels were most likely not this fragile or feminine in appearance, this set captures the sense of their joy.

The angels declared their joy by glorifying God and proclaiming peace on earth. In typical self-centered human fashion, we generally focus on the part that brings a promise to us—the peace on earth. We also generalize this promise to include all mankind, but the words actually confer the promise on "those with whom he is pleased." While global peace will ultimately result from this Child's work, in the meantime, internal peace—peace with God—is the immediate fulfillment of this proclamation. We best realize that promise when we turn our attention to the first part of the angel's message: giving glory to God.

December 18 – **See and Tell**

When the angels went away from them into heaven, the shepherds said to one another, "Let us go over to Bethlehem and see this thing that has happened, which the Lord has made known to us." And they went with haste and found Mary and Joseph, and the baby lying in a manger. And when they saw it, they made known the saying that had been told them concerning this child. And all who heard it wondered at what the shepherds told them. Luke 2:15-18

Nigeria

The shepherds responded to the astounding spectacle they had just witnessed by going immediately, without questioning what they had seen or heard. They believed what they had been told and set off to see for themselves. Their immediate response reminds me of those who Jesus later called—fishermen who left their nets, a tax collector who left his business. In Bethlehem the shepherds found everything just as the angel had described it: a newborn lying in a manger in a stable. After seeing the signs of the miraculous birth for themselves, they told others.

It seems strange that God chose shepherds as the group to witness the angelic visitation and the birth of the savior. In that society, they held such a negative reputation as a group that courts would not accept their testimony. Yet God chose this disreputable group as His witnesses. "For my thoughts are not your thoughts, neither are your ways my ways, declares the Lord" (Isaiah 55:8). God's confidence in these lowly witnesses seems to have been well placed, for they immediately began to let others know what had happened. Again, God did not choose those of high status or human credibility to accomplish His purpose but honored the poor and lowly esteemed as the first witnesses to the miracle of the incarnation.

Our roughly carved nativity set from Nigeria captures the sense of the humble circumstances into which the savior was born. The materials used to create the set remind us of the wood and straw in that Bethlehem stable, and of a humble group gathered in awe at seeing the sign that the angels described to them. Having seen, they went out and told others.

The Story continues to be passed along in this way, with those who have seen going and telling others. Today, people throughout the world have heard and believed the story, and the Good News continues to be proclaimed from Nazareth to New York to Nigeria.

December 19 – **A Time to Ponder**

But Mary treasured up all these things, pondering them in her heart.
Luke 2:19

Our first daughter was born in a Thai mission hospital. After giving birth in a modern, well-equipped delivery room, I was taken to the maternity ward where I shared a room with three Thai mothers—three Thai families, actually. Husbands camped on straw mats beneath the beds;

other family members came and went. My status as the ward's only foreigner elicited frank stares. Pulling the curtains around the bed for privacy only piqued the curiosity of the other occupants of the room, as they peered around the curtain to see what was going on. I soon learned that I aroused less attention if I simply left the curtains open.

As a Western woman raised as an only child, I supremely value privacy. Perhaps Mary would have been more comfortable than I in a communal setting, with family members going and coming. I wonder how she felt when her much-needed rest after a difficult journey and the exertions of childbirth was interrupted by the appearance of motley strangers gazing in wonder at her and her child. Did she wish they would go away and let her recover in peace or did she welcome this rough community in this setting so far from the community that would have surrounded her at home?

In any case, the visit from the shepherds surely gave her much to ponder. The shepherds no doubt told her and Joseph about the angelic visitors and their message. This confirmed to the couple the truth of God's promise that Mary would give birth to the long-awaited Savior Messiah.

Our Uzbek "Mary" bends over a traditional Central Asian cradle, thoughtfully contemplating her child, just as the mother of Jesus may have reflected on all that happened as she gazed at her newborn son. In contrast to the shepherds who went out spreading the word, Mary stored up all that she had seen and heard in her heart. Earlier in the narrative we hear of people responding "with haste"—Mary hurrying off to Bethlehem, the shepherds rushing off to check out the angel's proclamation—but now the time for contemplation had come, the time for processing and understanding the sequence of miracles over the past months. We may be grateful for the time that Mary took to ponder these events, for Luke likely learned about the birth of Jesus from her. Mary's witness, given over time, has impacted the world's understanding of Jesus' birth every bit as much, if not more, than the hasty telling of the shepherds. There is a place for both kinds of witness—the enthusiastic and immediate recounting of a particular event or a thoughtful remembrance of it after the passage of time.

December 20 – **Returning with Wonder**

And the shepherds returned, glorifying and praising God for all they had heard and seen, as it had been told them. Luke 2:20

During the years we lived in Mongolia, we traveled to Beijing at Christmas time to meet our daughters who flew in from boarding school in Malaysia. At that time Mongolia offered little in the way of shopping, so we enjoyed the comparative abundance of goods available in China. We especially liked to browse the rows of open stalls across the street from our hotel. In one of those shops, we found this hand painted porcelain set. As I unpack it from its bubble wrap storage each year, the set brings back memories of happy family times together.

Perhaps the two shepherds here are part of a family—father and son together witnessing the savior's birth. The younger shepherd carries a lamb, reminding us that the child in the manger is both the Lamb of God and the Good Shepherd. The shepherds' understanding of this child's identity may have been limited, but they understood enough to find reason to praise and glorify God.

Luke tells us that after seeing the child, the shepherds returned. They still had God-given responsibilities for tending their sheep, so they went back to their flocks. But what they had seen changed them. Their tedious and dreary tasks took on a sense of excitement as they glorified God. They clearly understood God as the source of the miraculous things they had seen, and they overflowed with worship and praise for Him.

We acknowledge Christmas as a time of great joy, bringing love and hope to our world. Yet in the midst of our daily responsibilities and the extra hustle and bustle of the Christmas season, how often do we pause to rejoice, glorifying and praising God as the shepherds did? I find that the music of Christmas often stimulates such a feeling of joy and praise in my heart. Many familiar carols, as well as more classical works, express well the wonder of the season. Bach's *Christians, Be Joyful* conveys an exhortation we might well take to heart as we listen.

The shepherds returned to their fields, but in their return, they retained the sense of joy and wonder at all they had heard and seen. Set aside some time during this busy season simply to rejoice.

December 21 – **Aliens and Astrology**

Now after Jesus was born in Bethlehem of Judea in the days of Herod the king, behold, wise men from the east came to Jerusalem, saying, "Where is he who has been born king of the Jews? For we saw his star when it rose and have come to worship him." Matthew 2:1-2

In the nativity story, God upsets our human expectations of an appropriate entrance to the world for His Son. His mother is a peasant woman, not a princess; His birthplace is in a stable, not a palace; and the first announcement of His birth is to shepherds, not religious leaders.

Now God uses astrology, a practice He has forbidden to His people, to reveal the birth of His Son to a group of Eastern Magi. As one commentary puts it, God "reveal(ed) himself where the pagans were looking." These pagans, having learned about the birth of a king, felt compelled to find him so that they could worship him. Matthew's first readers may have found it startling that God includes Gentiles in the first news of the savior's birth—and Gentiles about as alien as they could be—magicians far outside the realm of God's set-apart people.

The Magi learned of Jesus' birth from the stars, while the shepherds heard about it from the angels. The shepherds were looking for a savior; the wise men were searching for a king. Yet both groups responded with immediacy and belief and set out to find the newborn child.

In our travels in Central Asia, we found many figures that reminded us of the Magi. While the wise men are believed to have come from Persia, Matthew tells us only that they are "from the east." That could easily have included more distant places, such as Uzbekistan, from where these figures came. Two major cities along the Silk Route, Samarkand (also a center of the study of astronomy) and Bukhara, lie within the borders of modern-day Uzbekistan. In the Bukhara market, it is easy to envision caravans stopping for trade and fresh provisions. These terra cotta figures epitomize my mental image of the wise men. I love their bejeweled robes; similar costumes of velvet and gold are available today in Uzbek bazaars.

We expect that the Magi traveled by camel—or perhaps more accurately by dromedary. One of our cheerful beasts is a one-humped dromedary, the other, a two-humped Bactrian camel.

 Whatever their origins, these exotic caravans appeared on the Jerusalem streets looking for the newborn king. The Jewish establishment did not expect such visitors to herald the birth of their Messiah; nor were they aware that His birth had already occurred. The outsiders, aware that a spectacular event had taken place, came in faith, prepared to worship.

God may use surprising methods and choose surprising people to bring into His kingdom. We should not discount elements beyond our normal experiences, but instead prepare to learn faith lessons from unexpected sources.

December 22 – **A God-Honoring Response**

When Herod the king heard this, he was troubled, and all Jerusalem with him; and assembling all the chief priests and scribes of the people, he inquired of them where the Christ was to be born. They told him, "In Bethlehem of Judea, for so it is written by the prophet:

> *And you, O Bethlehem, in the land of Judah,*
> *are by no means least among the rulers of Judah;*
> *for from you shall come a ruler*
> *who will shepherd my people Israel."*

Then Herod summoned the wise men secretly and ascertained from them what time the star had appeared. And he sent them to Bethlehem, saying, "Go and search diligently for the child, and when you have found him, bring me word, that I too may come and worship him." Matthew 2:3-8

Matthew does not provide a specific country of origin for these wise men, describing them only as "from the East." Could they have come from present-day Afghanistan, Russia, or Tajikistan? Our figures from these countries embody our concept of wise men. We can easily imagine their caravan entering Jerusalem.

Caravans were nothing new for Jerusalem. They no doubt stirred some excitement whenever they arrived, but none had ever created the buzz that this one did. None had ever come before with the intent of worshipping a new king. No wonder they "troubled" Herod. Already prone to jealousy and paranoia, this new development would have caused him much dismay. "All Jerusalem" seemed troubled with him. Just predicting Herod's likely reaction would have created a sense of foreboding among the inhabitants of the city. Any additional fuel to increase his sense of paranoia could have disastrous repercussions.

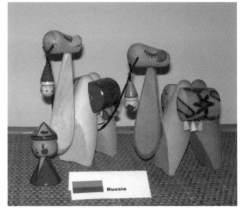

God provided supernatural guidance to the wise men in identifying the star and its meaning. The star led them to Jerusalem, but from there they needed assistance. So, they went to the place they thought most likely to give them the additional information they needed. But Herod, King of the Jews, had no more idea than these pagan astrologers. He turned to the religious community for help. These leaders referred to God's revelation through the Scriptures, explaining that the promised Messiah was to be born in Bethlehem.

We might expect that the religious leaders, hearing that the birth of a child in Bethlehem had attracted international attention, would want to see for themselves. But we hear nothing of any further interest from them or from the others in Jerusalem who had apparently been disturbed by the appearance of the Magi. The Jewish people who had been entrusted with the Scriptures and with God's promises showed little interest in the fulfillment of these promises.

Herod, on the other hand, showed great interest. The attention he paid to the matter was not feigned, but his desire to worship was. Herod believed the story, and rather than rejoice in the fulfilled promise, set out to annul it. He wanted no one to threaten his power—not even God Himself.

In this drama only the Magi, the outsiders, responded in a God-honoring way. They believed the revelation they had been given, sought for more direction from the Scriptures, and continued their journey so that they might worship.

We have the same options for responding to the Good News today: ignore it, resist it, or embrace it and worship.

December 23 - **What's Your Destination?**

After listening to the king, they went on their way. And behold, the star that they had seen when it rose went before them until it came to rest over the place where the child was. When they saw the star, they rejoiced exceedingly with great joy. Matthew 2:9-10

Thailand

Have you ever set out with a particular destination in mind—somewhere that you couldn't wait to be? How did you feel at the end of the journey? Excited? Exhausted? Fulfilled? Disappointed? Sometimes reaching the goal is rewarding; at other times, it's a letdown.

My first trip overseas was to Thailand, the origin of this nativity set. I felt a mixture of reactions on reaching that destination for the first time—relief, apprehension, excitement. In later years when we lived in other parts of Asia, returning to Thailand always gave me a feeling of joy in reaching a familiar place that I loved.

The Magi traveled a great distance to find a newborn king. Mostly the star led them; sometimes they sought assistance from those they presumed to be subjects of the new king. At last, the star rested over the place where the child was in Bethlehem, and "they rejoiced exceedingly with great joy." No disappointment here! In reaching their destination, the wise men felt a deep sense of joy. Here they found the star of Bethlehem resting over the Star that came out of Jacob, the bright Morning Star.

I feel something of that sense of joy when I return home from a long trip. In following the star, the wise men had found their true home as well. For Jesus is our home, and in finding Him, we reach Home.

December 24 – **Finding the Right Gift**

And going into the house they saw the child with Mary his mother, and they fell down and worshiped him. Then, opening their treasures, they offered him gifts, gold and frankincense and myrrh. Matthew 2:11

We often attribute the practice of gift-giving at Christmas to the example of the wise men who brought gifts to honor the newborn King. Most nativity sets, like this one from Honduras, include three wise men. Even though Matthew doesn't mention the number of visitors, it's commonly assumed to be three because of the three gifts mentioned: gold, frankincense, and myrrh. Not standard baby shower gifts, these offerings bear symbolic meaning appropriate to the child the wise men traveled so far to find. They had not come to see just any baby or to bring gifts chosen for cuteness or practicality but chosen to honor the King of Kings. They presented gold as a symbol of earthly kingship—a valuable gift given to show respect for the authority of the king. Frankincense, often used as a worship offering, symbolized the deity of the child. Myrrh signified the child's mortality and envisaged the suffering and death He would undergo.

The wise men were very aware of the significance of the child they had come to see, so as their first act on arrival, they worshipped Him. Only after falling down in worship did they open their treasures and produce the gifts, material indication of their heart's desire to honor Him.

We also relate our custom of gift giving at Christmas with God's gift of sending His Son. In an earlier post, I related traveling to Beijing at Christmas time to meet our daughters coming home from boarding school. At the end of their Christmas vacation, we sent the girls back to Malaysia from Beijing. While this always made me sad, I felt confident in their ability to navigate international travel as long as they were together. Once the older one graduated, though, our quiet younger daughter had to navigate the segment of the journey from Beijing to Bangkok on her own. I felt a sense of helplessness as I watched her head toward her plane in an airport that was far from user-friendly even for the savviest traveler. As I reflect on the nativity story today, I remember that feeling and wonder if God felt a similar sense of sadness watching His Son head toward earth. God, who knows all, certainly realized that earth was not the most reliable place for offering nurture and love. While He had provided a set of loving parents, God knew that the road ahead lay paved with sorrow and pain. Yet His love for us was so great, that God willingly sent His Son to bring us salvation.

The wise men understood the cosmic implications of the birth of this baby in Bethlehem. They responded by worshipping and bringing gifts. May our Christmas celebration include worship of Jesus, Savior and Christ, and may our gift giving include offering ourselves to Him.

December 25 – **Can You See?**

And at the end of eight days, when he was circumcised, he was called Jesus, the name given by the angel before he was conceived in the womb.

And when the time came for their purification according to the Law of Moses, they brought him up to Jerusalem to present him to the Lord (as it is written in the Law of the Lord, "Every male who first opens the womb shall be called holy to the Lord) and to offer a sacrifice according to what is said in the Law of the Lord, a pair of turtle doves, or two young pigeons." Now there was a man in Jerusalem whose name was Simeon, and this man was righteous and devout, waiting for the consolation of Israel, and the Holy Spirit was upon him. And it had been revealed to him by the Holy Spirit that he would not see death before he had seen the Lord's Christ. And he came in the Spirit into the temple, and when the parents brought in the child Jesus, to do for him according to the custom of the Law, he took him up in his arms and blessed God and said,

> *"Lord, now you are letting your servant depart in peace, according to your word;*
> *for my eyes have seen your salvation that you have prepared in the presence of all people,*
> *a light for revelation to the Gentiles, and for glory to your people Israel."*

And his father and his mother marveled at what was said about him. And Simeon blessed them and said to Mary his mother, "Behold, this child is appointed for the fall and rising of many in Israel, and for a sign that is opposed (and a sword will pierce through your own soul also), so that thoughts from many hearts may be revealed."
Luke 2:21-4

Mary and Joseph carefully carried out the requirements prescribed in the law for a firstborn son. On the eighth day after His birth, they had Him circumcised and named Him according to the angel's instructions. On the 40th day, they took Jesus to the temple for His dedication as the firstborn son and for Mary's ritual purification.

No doubt many other parents were there that day, bringing their offerings and dedicating newborns. Mary and Joseph appeared just like any other parents to most of the temple-goers, but one elderly man noticed something special about the baby they carried. Though his vision may have dimmed with age, his acute spiritual perception led Simeon to see the difference in this child. God had promised Simeon that he would see the Messiah before his death. Now His Spirit showed Simeon that the infant Jesus fulfilled that promise. Simeon's words of blessing as he held the baby include several references to light and sight: "my eyes have seen your salvation . . . a light for revelation to the Gentiles."

Our first nativity set, purchased at a Thai hilltribe sale decades ago, is constructed of burlap-covered cardboard. Burlap, the material of feed sacks, seems an appropriate fabric to represent a child born in a barn. But part of the figures' clothing is velvet—the fabric of royalty—a fitting combination to clothe a servant king. When Mary and Joseph presented Jesus at the temple, casual observers saw just a child born in humble circumstances. Only those whom God blessed with special sight saw the complete picture—the fulfillment of the promised King and Messiah and a source of blessing to the world.

How acute is your vision as you celebrate this child's birth today? Do you see a romanticized version of a baby's birth, a sweet story whitewashed from the dirt and pain and tears actually entailed? Or do you see the birth of the King of Kings, God clothing Himself in flesh, taking on our pain to bring salvation? Thank God for the illumination He provides to those willing to see Him with open eyes.

December 26 – Waiting for Consolation

And there was a prophetess, Anna, the daughter of Phanuel, of the tribe of Asher. She was advanced in years, having lived with her husband seven years from when she was a virgin, and then as a widow until she was eighty-four. She did not depart from the temple, worshipping with fasting and prayer night and day. And coming up at that very hour she began to give thanks to God and to speak of him to all who were waiting for the redemption of Jerusalem.

THAILAND

And when they had performed everything according to the Law of the Lord, they returned into Galilee, to their own town of Nazareth. And the child grew and became strong, filled with wisdom. And the favor of God was upon him. Luke 2:36-40

Anna had been married just seven years when her husband died, leaving her a young, vulnerable widow. With limited options, she chose one close to her heart—to spend as much time as possible in the temple, worshiping God as she waited for the promised consolation of Israel. That had been many decades ago, and now, as an old woman, she still waited.

Our Thai wood carving depicts a family unit of father, mother, and child. No facial features set them apart from any other family anywhere. Their clothing suggests a certain time and place, and those of us with a Christian heritage "recognize" them as Jesus and His parents. But like this anonymous carving, Mary and Joseph and their infant did not stand out from among the other families who had come to the temple to fulfill the requirements of the law. No halo encircled the baby's head.

Yet God revealed to Simeon and Anna that this was not just any 40-day-old baby, but the very consolation they'd been waiting for. As a prophetess, Anna began telling like-minded others that their wait was over.

Anna was old, a woman, and a widow—a person considered of little value in her society. Yet she gained respect by spending time in the temple, completely dedicated to worship. She fits the Psalmist's description of a righteous person:

> *They are planted in the house of the Lord;*
> *   they flourish in the courts of our God.*
> *They still bear fruit in old age;*
> *   they are ever full of sap and green.* Psalm 92:13-14

I do not want to be described as "sappy," but without life-giving sap, a tree could not flourish. If that's what I need to flourish, so be it. Anna's story tells us our life still has purpose beyond our allotted "three-score-and-ten." We are never too old to worship and glorify God, the very purpose for which He created us. In fact, as physical limitations narrow the margins of our world, we may even be freer to focus on God, and in the process, experience surprising consolations.

December 27 – Out of Egypt

Now when they [the wise men] had departed, behold, an angel of the Lord appeared to Joseph in a dream and said, "Rise, take the child and his mother, and flee to Egypt, and remain there until I tell you, for Herod is about to search for the child, to destroy him." And he rose and took the child and his mother by night and departed to Egypt and remained there until the death of Herod. This was to fulfill what the Lord had spoken by the prophet, "Out of Egypt I called my son." Matthew 2:13-15

CROATIA

One long-ago December, we traveled with our two-month-old daughter in our pick-up truck into Northern Thailand to visit two remote refugee camps. Our journey took us over jungle-covered mountains to an unfamiliar area. As night fell, we realized we wouldn't make our destination of a colleague's home. We began to look for a place to stay. Few towns lay along the route; the first one we came to had no hotel. On that dark Christmas Eve, I began to identify with Mary and Joseph as they traveled toward Bethlehem and later toward Egypt.

Yet our plight bore little resemblance to the dangers they faced, particularly as they fled the wrath of a tyrannical king. Nor did it compare to the journeys of the refugees we would be visiting who had fled their country on foot, hiding in the jungle to escape the pursuit of armed soldiers. Now, after over four decades, the worldwide flow of refugees from danger in their home countries has only increased.

Our Croatian nativity sculpture, with the image of the Holy Family emerging from a rock's rough surface, reminds me of promises Joseph must have clung to:

> *The Lord is my rock and my fortress and my deliverer, my God, my rock, in whom I take refuge, my shield, and the horn of my salvation, my stronghold.* Psalm 18:2

Joseph had learned to trust his dreams, and he had clear instructions for securing Jesus' safety. These instructions, and his faith in God his rock, gave him the confidence to obey the angel. We know nothing about the journey, only that it was successful. Jesus began His life not only among the poor, but among the homeless and refugees. We may not be called to identify with the oppressed to the extent that Jesus did, but we certainly can listen for God's voice in their cries.

December 28 – Weeping and Lamentation

Then Herod, when he saw that he had been tricked by the wise men, became furious, and he sent and killed all the male children in Bethlehem and in all that region who were two years old or under, according to the time that he had ascertained from the wise men. Then was fulfilled what was spoken by the prophet Jeremiah:

> *"A voice was heard in Ramah,*
> *weeping and loud lamentation,*
> *Rachel weeping for her children;*
> *she refused to be comforted, because they are no more."*

Matthew 2:16-18

We do not like to think about this part of the story at Christmas time—or any time, for that matter. We prefer to focus on the birth of an innocent baby and the joy proclaimed on heaven and earth. We wish the story of King Herod's slaughter of boy babies hadn't happened—not just because of its horror for those it impacted, but also because it forces us to acknowledge the reality of evil in the world.

Our nativity set from Cambodia seems an appropriate one to pair with this passage. In the 1970's, the evil Khmer Rouge regime killed one of every four Cambodians. Those who survived suffered incredibly. HIV/AIDS has since killed many more, making orphans of hundreds of thousands of children. Large numbers of Cambodians still live in a state of PTSD.

In my own country, the words "Uvalde" and "Sandy Hook" recall the senseless killing of young children. We recoil in horror when we hear such things and declare we "have no words." Jeremiah's words, quoted by Matthew above, express the sense of complete desolation a mother feels at the senseless death of her child. What relevance does the story of a baby's birth have to this kind of suffering?

Such events—Bethlehem, Cambodia, Sandy Hook—show us that evil exists. We respond in horror. We question why God would allow such a thing. For me, the story we celebrate at Christmas comes closest to offering an answer I can begin to grasp. God came Himself to live among us, fully aware that would involve suffering and death. The God Who shares our sorrow will ultimately overcome evil. Pray for the hastening of the day when Jesus overcomes death and evil.

December 29 – The Carpenter's Son

But when Herod died, behold, an angel of the Lord appeared in a dream to Joseph in Egypt, saying, "Rise, take the child and his mother and go to the land of Israel, for those who sought the child's life are dead." And he rose and took the child and his mother and went to the land of Israel. But when he heard that Archelaus was reigning over Judea in place of his father Herod, he was afraid to go there, and being warned in a dream he withdrew to the district of Galilee. And he went and lived in a city called Nazareth, so that what was spoken by the prophets might be fulfilled, that he would be called a Nazarene. Matthew 3:19-23

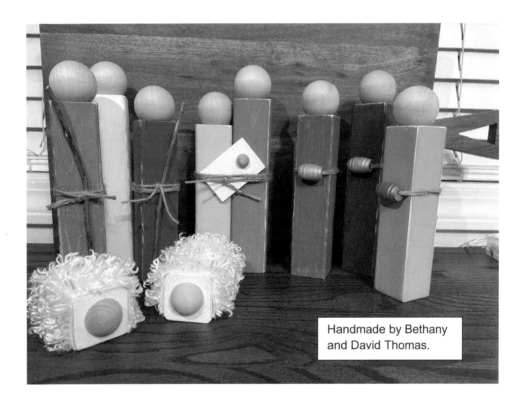

Handmade by Bethany and David Thomas.

Again, Joseph followed his dreams. Not the egocentric "follow your dreams" philosophy we so often hear, but rather obedience to God's direction. God used dreams as His language of communication with Joseph. People today still hear from God in this way, though not as commonly in the Western world. Most of us sense God's leading through Scripture or the counsel of wise friends or circumstances God orders in our lives.

God's direction took Joseph to Egypt and back and ultimately to his hometown of Nazareth. At that time, Nazareth was a small, despised village, a place about which Nathanael asked, "Can anything good come out of Nazareth?" (John 1:46). Here Jesus spent His childhood and learned carpentry skills from Joseph. I find it difficult to grasp how the One who spoke trees into being submitted Himself to learning to shape wood into useful items.

Our daughter and son-in-law created the nativity set pictured here, using simple blocks of wood. Our son-in-law's carpentry skills extend to his ability to create their family's dining room table and chairs. Anyone like him who has worked with wood has experienced some of the sensations Jesus would have felt in learning the carpentry trade and enjoying the satisfaction of a well-made finished product. Man, made in the image of a Creator God, shares God's attribute of creativity. I appreciate that the Creator of the universe began His adult years on earth as a man learning a creative trade.

To me, the blocks of wood in this set represent Nazareth's reputation—despised pieces too small to be of use in any major construction project yet fashioned into symbolic portrayals of an earth-changing story. Jesus' origins in a despised town did not keep Him from fulfilling the great purpose God had for Him. No matter how lowly—or even how lofty—your background, God will not allow that to thwart His purpose for your life.

December 30 – Jesus the Word

In the beginning was the Word, and the Word was with God, and the Word was God. John 1:1

NIGERIA

John begins his gospel much earlier in time than either Matthew or Luke— "in the beginning." These words, reflecting the very first words of Genesis, indicate that Jesus existed long before the angel announced His birth to Mary. In fact, He existed even *before* the beginning. He was already there "in the beginning."

John refers to Jesus as "the Word." He tells us that Jesus was not only with God in the beginning but was God Himself.

Jesus, God made man, represents one way God communicates with us. We speak of Jesus as "the Living Word" and of the Bible as "the written Word." While terms like "body language" and "non-verbal communication" describe some of the ways we express ourselves to others, our most effective means of communication require words.

If you want to tell a friend something, how do you go about it? This probably depends on your age. Those of us who have been around longer probably want to see our friend in person and give our news face-to-face. Younger people might send a quick text. God uses both means of communication. He sent Jesus as our in-person communicator, and He gave us the Bible as our text message. Because we do not live in the time and place of Jesus, our way of listening to Jesus now comes primarily through the written Word.

Folded up, our crudely carved Nigerian triptych looks like a giant pencil. Pencils are the first instruments we give children when teaching them to write. Children have already learned to use their spoken words to communicate; a pencil enables them to use written words as well. The tiny figure of a baby wrapped in twine lies embedded in our Nigerian "pencil," just as the story of Jesus lies at the core of God's written Word. Have we begun to grasp the significance that the Lord of the universe has gone to such lengths to communicate with us?

December 31 – Jesus the Creator

He was in the beginning with God. All things were made through him, and without him was not any thing made that was made. John 1:2-3

Matthew begins his gospel with Jesus' human pedigree; Luke begins with the pregnancies of Elizabeth and Mary. These tell us about Jesus the man. But John wants us to understand that the man Jesus is also the eternal God. He existed before the creation of the world, and, with His Father, spoke our world into being. Nothing exists that was not made by Jesus— not flowers, trees, or seas; not elephants, wrens, or men; not mountains, plains or rain; not light or night. Even the elements we use to create modern buildings, medicines, and machines—He created ALL things. That includes making humankind in the image of the Creator God.

When God finished creating the world, He "saw everything that He had made, and behold, it was very good" (Genesis 1:31). Can you identify with that feeling? God endowed us with the ability to feel pleasure in creating and to experience joy in the finished product. Few of us are great artists, but all of us can create something good that brings us satisfaction.

My husband and I began working with refugees in Thailand after the end of the Vietnam War. We observed that even among those who had lost virtually everything in their flight toward freedom, many of the women occupied themselves with traditional needlework. In the dirty, barren, refugee camps, women created lovely textile art. We began a project to help them market these crafts, a project that later migrated into Laos where poor village women still earn money to help their families, while experiencing the satisfaction of making something beautiful.

Many of the refugees from Laos were members of the Hmong ethnic group. In the camps, they began creating representational art, along with their traditional cross-stitch embroidery and reverse applique. At first, these images portrayed their recent experiences in fleeing danger, but before long, they began creating representations of village life. A few years ago, I saw the first embroidered nativity scene, a motif they have now incorporated into their regular repertoire.

Like this wall hanging, most nativity sets in our collection are handmade. I trust the creators of these sets achieved a sense of satisfaction in making them. Their creativity continues to bring me joy as I unwrap and display the sets each year.

January 1 – The Light of the World

In him was life, and the life was the light of men. The light shines in the darkness, and the darkness has not overcome it.

There was a man sent from God, whose name was John. He came as a witness, to bear witness about the light, that all might believe through him. He was not the light, but came to bear witness about the light.

The true light, which gives light to everyone, was coming into the world. John 1:4-9

In His first creative word, God called forth light, giving visibility to the rest of His created works. We rely on physical light to navigate our way in the material world, as we rely on Jesus for spiritual light.

Today, most countries in the world acknowledge the commercial aspects of Christmas, displaying colorful lights and Christmas trees. When we first went overseas in 1975, this was not yet true in Thailand. But the beloved King Rama IX's birthday fell in December, and Bangkok decorated for the celebration with strings of lights. This seemed appropriate as we simultaneously commemorated the birth of the King of Kings. Since Christmas decorations weren't plentiful, I decorated our home primarily with candles. I loved the simplicity and symbolism of their bright flames.

Our angel candleholders come from Bangladesh and Indonesia. Though Christians make up a minority in these countries; nevertheless, their presence indicates that the good news proclaimed by the angels has been shared with many of the world's peoples. The message the angels proclaimed to the shepherds continues to bring light and joy to a dark world.

Have you noticed how much brighter a candle flame appears at night than it does in the daytime? Or perhaps you've bought a flashlight and want to test how bright it is. Clicking it on in the daytime gives you little indication of how well it will work at night unless you go into a windowless room and close the door. There the contrast of light and darkness shows you the power of the flashlight. The power of the flashlight remains the same, but we see it best in the dark.

In the same way, the presence of Jesus is always with us, but we may sense it more clearly in the darkness. We accord symbolic value to celebrating the birth of Jesus during the darkest days of the year in the Northern Hemisphere. If we struggle to feel celebratory at this time of year when we find ourselves facing difficult circumstances, we can still reach toward the light of the world who came to illuminate our darkness. The glory of the Lord brought light to a dark Bethlehem night and continues to shine today in dark places, whether geographical or emotional.

January 2 – The Father's Children

He was in the world, and the world was made through him, yet the world did not know him. He came to his own, and his own people did not receive him. But to all who did receive him, who believed in his name, he gave the right to become children of God, who were born, not of blood nor of the will of the flesh nor of the will of man, but of God. John 1:10-13

When Jesus was born into the world He had created, most people did not believe who He was. Some of those people eventually killed Him. Ever since, many who have believed Jesus' claims about Himself, have found that there are those who want to kill them.

On Easter Sunday, 2019, a Sunday School teacher in Sri Lanka asked his class of children, "How many of you are willing to die for Christ?" All the children raised their hands and lit candles to show their sincerity. A few minutes later, as they walked to their church service, an explosion triggered by a suicide bomber killed half of them. Altogether, suicide bombers killed nearly 300 Sri Lankan Christians that day. Though this kind of attack is unusual in that country, the Christian minority does suffer for their faith.

Believing that Jesus created the world and is one with God can lead to danger; but God offers recompense for those who believe. He rewards us by making us His children. As Jesus would later tell Nicodemus, we enter this relationship through a new birth. As God's children, we have eternal life. Jesus' enemies killed Him, but God raised Him from the dead. Those Sri Lankan children who died on that Easter Sunday will one day rise again as well.

Jesus came into the world as part of a human family, with a mother and father and sisters and brothers. In doing so, He invites us to be born into His kingdom family and offers us relationship as children of His heavenly Father.

January 3 – The Word Became Flesh

And the Word became flesh and dwelt among us, and we have seen his glory, glory as of the only Son from the Father, full of grace and truth. (John bore witness about him, and cried out, "This was he of whom I said, 'He who comes after me ranks before me, because he was before me.'") For from his fullness we have all received, grace upon grace. For the law was given through Moses; grace and truth came through Jesus Christ. No one has ever seen God; the only God, who is at the Father's side, he has made him known. John 1:14-18

UNITED STATES

The Apostle John refers to Jesus as "the Word." John writes that Jesus became flesh, taking on muscle and fat, the substance of humanity. The theological term for this is "incarnation." God with us, *Emmanuel.* How better to be with us than to become like us?

While muscle and fat make up the literal components of human flesh, the Bible uses the metaphor of dust to describe what we are made of. Genesis 2:7 says, "then the Lord God formed the man of dust from the ground and breathed into his nostrils the breath of life, and the man became a living creature." The elements that make up our bodies are elements also found in the earth's dust. And dead cells from our bodies continually add to that dust. (Up to half the dust in our homes consists of human skin cells!) As God told Adam, "you are dust, and to dust you shall return." Abraham referred to himself as "dust and ashes" (Genesis 18:27), the traditional substances signaling mourning or repentance.

Ashes from the volcanic eruption of Mount St. Helen's form the nativity set featured today. The sculptor took an unattractive substance, a product of massive disruption, and formed it into a representation of humanity at its loveliest—the baby Jesus.

In Isaiah 61:3, the prophet spoke of beauty replacing ashes. Jesus read the first part of this Isaiah passage to the synagogue at Nazareth at the very beginning of His ministry.

> *The Spirit of the Lord is upon me,*
> *because he has anointed me*
> *to proclaim good news to the poor.*
> *He has sent me to proclaim liberty to the captives*
> *and recovering of sight to the blind,*
> *to set at liberty those who are oppressed,*
> *to proclaim the year of the Lord's favor.*
> (Luke 4:18-19, quoting from Isaiah 61)

In reading these words, Jesus announced His ministry of "grace and truth," clothed in human flesh, proclaiming the glory of His Father.

January 4 – A Voice in the Wilderness

And this is the testimony of John, when the Jews sent priests and Levites from Jerusalem to ask him, "Who are you?" He confessed, and did not deny, but confessed, "I am not the Christ." And they asked him, "What then? Are you Elijah?" He said, "I am not." "Are you the Prophet?" And he answered, "No." So they said to him, "Who are you? We need to give an answer to those who sent us. What do you say about yourself?" He said, "I am the voice of one crying out in the wilderness, 'Make straight the way of the Lord,' as the prophet Isaiah said."

(Now they had been sent from the Pharisees.) They asked him, "Then why are you baptizing, if you are neither the Christ, nor Elijah, nor the Prophet?" John answered them, "I baptize with water, but among you stands one you do not know, even he who comes after me, the strap of whose sandal I am not worthy to untie." These things took place in Bethany across the Jordan, where John was baptizing. John 1:19-28

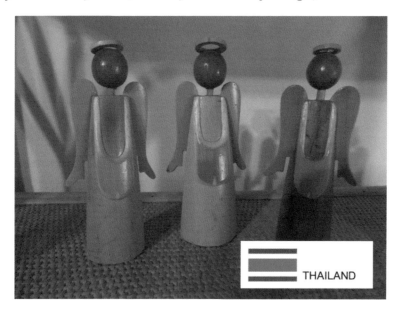

THAILAND

We last read about Jesus' cousin John when he was an infant, and his father, Zechariah, affirmed that his son's name should be John. Upon that affirmation, Zechariah regained his voice that had been silent throughout Elizabeth's pregnancy. In today's passage, the Apostle John presents John the Baptist as a grown man facing the question from Jewish leaders: "Who are you?"

In response, John basically answered, "I am the voice." How ironic that formerly mute Zechariah's son personified the Voice proclaiming the Messiah! Once Zechariah found his voice, he began proclaiming the news that his son John later echoed.

Other voices that proclaimed the Messiah included angels, messengers to Zechariah, Mary, and the shepherds. Our angelic chorus pictured here was formed from bamboo in Thailand. As a type of grass, bamboo illustrates a further point that Isaiah made in prophesying the voice that would announce the Messiah:

> A voice says, "Cry!"
>   And I said, "What shall I cry?"
> All flesh is grass,
>   and all its beauty is like the flower of the field.
> The grass withers, the flower fades
>   when the breath of the Lord blows on it;
>   surely the people are grass.
> The grass withers, the flower fades,
>   but the word of our God will stand forever. (Isaiah 40:6-8)

While an unusually sturdy grass, bamboo nevertheless ultimately fades. Some species take over 100 years to flower. Once they do, the plant declines and usually dies. In contrast to flesh and grass, God's Word is eternal. That includes Jesus, God's Living Word.

January 5 – The Lamb of God

The next day he saw Jesus coming toward him, and said, "Behold, the Lamb of God, who takes away the sin of the world! This is he of whom I said, 'After me comes a man who ranks before me, because he was before me.' I myself did not know him, but for this purpose I came baptizing with water, that he might be revealed to Israel." And John bore witness: "I saw the Spirit descend from heaven like a dove, and it remained on him. I myself did not know him, but he who sent me to baptize with water said to me, 'He on whom you see the Spirit descend and remain, this is he who baptizes with the Holy Spirit.' And I have seen and have borne witness that this is the Son of God." John 1: 29-34

Most of our nativity sets contain lambs or sheep. This set from Kazakhstan not only includes sheep, but its creators also fashioned it from felt, a product of sheep's wool. In Central Asia, where felt making originated, people use felt in everything from clothing to the insulating covering for yurts, their traditional dwellings. (The little round structure on the left is a miniature yurt—the elements of this set are not made to scale!) Shepherding is as vital to Central Asian culture as it was to Israel at the time of Jesus' birth.

John the Baptist introduces Jesus as "the Lamb of God, who takes away the sin of the world!" Those of us raised in the Christian faith understand this allusion right away, but it might have presented a mystery to the Jews speaking with John. The Old Testament contains no direct reference to the Lamb of God, though Isaiah's prophecies hint at the link between the Messiah and a sacrificial lamb.[1] New Testament Christians understood this idea more clearly in retrospect as they connected Jesus' death with the Passover lamb whose blood protected the firstborn sons of Jewish households in Egypt. Today, we associate Jesus' identity as the Lamb of God with His sacrificial death on the cross. The Apostle John referenced Jesus as the Lamb not only in the verses above, but also extensively in Revelation. Paul[2] and Peter[3] also referred to Him this way.

A sheep doesn't have to die to offer its wool for felt making. God's Lamb, however, did offer His life. At the time John the Baptist presented Jesus as the Lamb of God, he may not have understood this implication of the title. But he recognized God's Spirit descending on Jesus as a sign that Jesus would baptize with the Holy Spirit. In this introduction to the Trinity, John affirms Jesus' identity as God's beloved Son.

---

[1] *He was oppressed, and he was afflicted, yet he opened not his mouth; like a lamb that is led to the slaughter, and like a sheep that before its shearers is silent, so he opened not his mouth.* Isaiah 53:7

[2] *For Christ, our Passover lamb, has been sacrificed.* I Corinthians 5:7

[3] *but with the precious blood of Christ, like that of a lamb without blemish or spot.* I Peter 1:19

January 6 – Epiphany

On the third day there was a wedding at Cana in Galilee, and the mother of Jesus was there. Jesus also was invited to the wedding with his disciples. When the wine ran out, the mother of Jesus said to him, "They have no wine." And Jesus said to her, "Woman, what does this have to do with me? My hour has not yet come." His mother said to the servants, "Do whatever he tells you."

Now there were six stone water jars there for the Jewish rites of purification, each holding twenty or thirty gallons. Jesus said to the servants, "Fill the jars with water." And they filled them up to the brim. And he said to them, "Now draw some out and take it to the master of the feast." So they took it. When the master of the feast tasted the water now become wine, and did not know where it came from (though the servants who had drawn the water knew), the master of the feast called the bridegroom and said to him, "Everyone serves the good wine first, and when people have drunk freely, then the poor wine. But you have kept the good wine until now." This, the first of his signs, Jesus did at Cana in Galilee, and manifested his glory. And his disciples believed in him. John 2:1-11

Many Christian traditions celebrate Epiphany on January 6. For some, the celebration focuses primarily on the visit of the Magi to the baby Jesus; others include two additional events: Jesus' baptism and His first miracle. These events reveal Jesus as God's Son, the long-awaited Messiah, offering an epiphany—a revelation—of Jesus' identity.

Today's passage describes the miracle at Cana. I've paired this story with figures we bought in Tajikistan. We couldn't find an actual nativity set in this Muslim country, so we bought a group of little wooden figures that includes a couple musicians. I can imagine them providing music for a Tajik wedding. Traditional Tajik weddings last several days, with music, dancing and feasting. The wedding that Jesus attended in Cana would have had more resemblance to a Tajik wedding than to my own simple ceremony with a quiet cake-and-punch reception in a church basement afterwards! One of the similarities would have been the significant financial impact the ceremony had on the family. In 2017, the Tajik government imposed a law limiting the length and size of the ceremony to keep families from going into debt from wedding spending.

The family at Cana faced this problem. They provided to the best of their financial ability, and still their provision proved inadequate. Running out of wine would create an unimaginable loss of face for the family and put the newly married couple in an awkward social position. Jesus' first miracle didn't just give the wedding guests a taste of fine wine; it saved a friend's family from social disgrace. More importantly, the miracle evidenced Jesus' glory and caused His disciples to believe in Him.

It feels meaningful to conclude our Advent and Christmas meditations with the story of a wedding. We have looked back on events occurring when Jesus entered humanity; a wedding draws us forward to the day when we will be part of the glorious celebration of the Wedding Feast of the Lamb, when the Church becomes Christ's bride.

ABOUT THE COVER

I photographed a wood carving from Mongolia to create the image used for the cover of this book. This carving is "one of my favorite things." Not only do I love its elegantly simple design, but running my hands over its smoothly textured surface also brings me joy. The silky feeling against my fingertips somehow imparts a soothing and calming sensation. The skilled artist who created the piece's visual beauty must have worked patiently and persistently to apply the pressure needed to create such smoothness.

As the piece hangs on our wall during the Christmas season, one would never guess the contrast hidden on its back side. If you turn it over, it appears that the wood was once used as a cutting board. The back is sliced with thin, dark grooves, an ugly contrast to the visual and tactile loveliness of the front. These random lines remind me of the word "stripes" sometimes used in the Bible to describe the scars left from a beating. Such wounds covered the back of our Savior as He hung on the cross. These are the "stripes" by which we are healed.

Most of us bear scars of some kind from past experiences. Like the back of the picture, we hide them from view. But we don't have to bear these permanently. It was for such pain that Jesus incurred His own suffering—so that ours might be redeemed and healed.

I appreciate the message of our Mongolian wood carving. The front displays the beauty of the nativity story—of God become man as a lovely, innocent baby; and the back tells the rest of the story—of the suffering that Man would one day undergo on our behalf.

But he was wounded for our transgressions, he was bruised for our iniquities: the chastisement of our peace was upon him; and with his stripes we are healed. Isaiah 53:5 (KJV)

ABOUT THE AUTHOR

JEAN CASKEY ANDRIANOFF grew up as a "PK" (preacher's kid), living in California, Nebraska, and Pennsylvania. After she graduated from Geneva College, God took her and her husband, David, to Thailand, Laos, Mongolia, and Malaysia over a twenty-five-year period of ministry under the Christian and Missionary Alliance and World Concern. They now live on the Olympic Peninsula in Washington State, where Jean finds inspiration for writing from God's creation, family, life experiences, and her faith in Jesus. David and Jean have two daughters and three grandchildren.

Jean is the author of *Chosen for a Special Joy*, the story of David's parents and a people movement to Christ among the Hmong of Laos, and *They Sailed to Cyprus*, the account of her father's ministry on the Island of Cyprus during the period between the World Wars. She developed a Sunday School curriculum for the Lao church that has been widely used in Cambodia as well. A translated version of her *Story of Souphine* was published in Laos.

Printed in Great Britain
by Amazon

31241943R00050